BE THE BRIGHT ONE

52 WEEKS OF GOD'S LIGHT AND HEART TRANSFORMATION"

Copyright © 2025

All rights reserved.

This is a work of nonfiction. All characters and descriptions of events are the product of the author's imagination and any resemblance to actual persons is entirely coincidental.
The information in this book expresses the author's views and opinions and does not necessarily represent the views of any organization.

First published 2025

TABLE OF CONTENTS

Week 1: God Made You to Shine 1

Week 2: Shine from the Inside Out 3

Week 3: God's Light Grows in You 5

Week 4: Let Your Light Shine Everywhere 7

Week 5: Kindness Starts with You 11

Week 6: The Power of a Kind Word 13

Week 7: The Forgiveness 15

Week 8: Kindness in Action 17

Week 9: Rooted in God's Word 21

Week 10: Patience in the Waiting 23

Week 11: Growing Through Challenges 26

Week 12: Grateful Hearts Grow Bright 29

Week 13: Filled with God's Love 33

Week 14: The Power of a Loving Heart 35

Week 15: Forgive and Shine 38

Week 16: Loving the Unlovable 40

Week 17: Shine Through Helping Hands 42

Week 18: Speak Love Everywhere You Go 44

Week 19: Love That Listens 46

Week 20: When God Is Quiet 48
Week 21: Joy Comes from Jesus 51
Week 22: Don't Let Anyone Steal Your Joy 55
Week 23: Joy Through Praise 57
Week 24: Let Your Joy Shine! 59
Week 25: Be Still and Feel God's Peace 62
Week 26: Be a Peacemaker 64
Week 27: Trusting God Step by Step 66
Week 28: Faith While You Wait 68
Week 29: When Plans Change 70
Week 30: When I Feel Weak, God Is Strong 73
Week 31: Shine with Courage 75
Week 32: Standing Strong in Faith 77
Week 33: Say What You Believe 79
Week 34: Joy in the Journey 81
Week 35: Let Joy Spread! 83
Week 36: Peace in My Heart 85
Week 37: Peace on the Inside 88
Week 38: Peace Through Prayer 90
Week 39: Peace That Stays 92
Week 40: Sharing God's Peace 95

Week 41: The Beauty of a Quiet Heart 98
Week 42: The Power of Listening to God's Voice 100
Week 43: Walking in God's Way 102
Week 44: Faith Even When It's Hard 104
Week 45: God's Promises Never Fail 106
Week 46: Trusting God in Every Moment 108
Week 47: Courage to Step Out in Faith 110
Week 48: Shining Bright Through Challenges 112
Week 49: Peace in God's Presence 114
Week 50: Joy in the Quiet Moments 117
Week 51: Faith That Endures 119
Week 52: Shine On! 121

WEEK 1
GOD MADE YOU TO SHINE

Bible Verse:
"You are the light of the world—like a city on a hill that cannot be hidden."
— Matthew 5:14 (NLT)

Reflection:
God made you special, bright, and full of His light! Just like the sun lights up the sky, your smile, kindness, and love can bring light to the people around you. Sometimes the world feels dark — people might be sad, lonely, or afraid. But when you share God's love through your words and actions, you make the world brighter.

Remember, shining for God doesn't mean being perfect — it means letting His love
show in everything you do.

Heart Lesson:
God's light is already inside you. You don't have to try hard to shine — just love others the way He loves you.

GOD MADE YOU TO SHINE

Action Challenge:
Do one thing this week that shows God's love.

Example: Help someone, share a toy, give a compliment, or say a prayer for a friend.

Prayer:
Dear God, thank You for filling me with Your light. Help me to shine bright and show Your love everywhere I go. Amen.

WEEK 2
SHINE FROM THE INSIDE OUT

Bible Verse:
"People look at the outside of a person, but the Lord looks at the heart."
— 1 Samuel 16:7 (ICB)

Heart Talk:
Sometimes we try really hard to look nice, do well in school, or make people like us. But God isn't watching how perfect your clothes are or how many stars you get on your paper — He's looking at your heart.

When your heart is full of love, kindness, and honesty, that's when you shine brightest! God's light begins inside you — and when you let Him fill your heart, others can see it in your smile, your words, and your actions.

Think and Shine:

When do you feel closest to God?

What makes your heart feel bright and full of love?

Is there something this week you can do to make someone else's heart feel happy too?

SHINE FROM THE INSIDE OUT

Action Challenge:
Each morning, before you start your day, whisper a little prayer: God, fill my heart with Your light today.
Then, try to show that light wherever you go at home, at school, or on the playground.

Prayer:
Dear God, thank You for seeing my heart. Please help me keep it full of Your love and shine from the inside out. Amen.

WEEK 3
GOD'S LIGHT GROWS IN YOU

Bible Verse:
"Let your roots grow down into Him, and let your lives be built on Him."
— Colossians 2:7 (NLT)

Reflection:
Think about a tiny seed. It starts small — hidden in the dirt — but with sunlight, water, and care, it grows into something beautiful.

That's how God's light grows in you! Every time you pray, listen to His Word, or show kindness, your light grows stronger.

You might not notice it right away, but others will see the difference — in your smile, your words, and your heart.

Creative Activity: "My Growing Light"
You'll need:
A sheet of paper
Crayons, markers, or colored pencils

GOD'S LIGHT GROWS IN YOU

Step 1:
Draw a big flower or tree.

Step 2:
Inside the flower or along the branches, write or draw ways you can let God's light grow in you — like being kind, forgiving, praying, helping, being thankful.

Step 3:
Hang your drawing somewhere you can see it all week.
Each time you look at it, remember: God's light is growing in me!

Heart Lesson:
Even small acts of faith help God's light grow stronger in your heart. Keep watering it with love!

Prayer:
Dear God, thank You for planting Your light in my heart. Help me care for it so it grows bright and strong every day. Amen.

WEEK 4
LET YOUR LIGHT SHINE EVERYWHERE

Bible Verse:
"Let your light shine before others, that they may see your good deeds and glorify your Father in heaven." — Matthew 5:16 (NIV)

Reflection:
God didn't give you His light to keep it hidden — He gave it to share!

Every time you do something kind, help someone, or speak gently, your light shines brighter. Some people may never read a Bible, but they can see God's love when they look at how you live.

Your smile, your kindness, your patience — those are the ways you tell the world, "God's love is here!"

Shine Challenge of the Week:
This week, pick one big way to show God's light.

Here are some ideas:

Write a note or draw a picture to cheer someone up.

LET YOUR LIGHT SHINE EVERYWHERE

Where can you shine your light this week—at home, school, or with a friend who needs it most?

Help your parents or teachers without being asked.

Invite a lonely classmate to play or sit with you.

Say something kind to someone who seems sad.

After you do it, write or draw how it felt in your journal.

Ask yourself: Did I feel God's light shining through me?

Heart Lesson:
When you share God's love, your heart gets brighter — and you help others feel His love too.

Prayer:
Dear God, thank You for trusting me to carry Your light. Show me ways to shine for You every day and make the world brighter with Your love. Amen.

LET YOUR LIGHT SHINE EVERYWHERE

A Bright Story from Miss Susan: God's Light in You

When I was a little girl, I loved lighting candles during family prayer time. I remember how one tiny flame could fill the whole room with a soft, golden glow. I used to think, How can something so small make such a big difference?

One night, during a power outage, I carried my candle down the hallway. The house was dark and quiet, but that small flame helped everyone see where to go. My mom smiled and said, "See, Susan? That's what God's light in you does—it helps others find their way."

That stayed in my heart. As I grew older, I realized that every kind word, every prayer, every moment of love is like lighting a candle in someone's darkness. You don't have to be the biggest, loudest, or most popular to shine for God. You just have to be willing to glow where He's placed you.

So whenever you feel small or unnoticed, remember this: even the tiniest light changes the darkness. God's light in you was never meant to hide—it was meant to shine!

LET YOUR LIGHT SHINE EVERYWHERE

Reflection Question:
Where can you shine your light this week—at home, school, or with a friend who needs it most?

WEEK 5
KINDNESS STATRTS WITH YOU

Bible Verse:
"Those who are kind benefit themselves, but the cruel bring ruin on themselves." — Proverbs 11:17 (NIV)

Story Reflection:

One sunny morning, Mia was getting ready for school. Her little brother spilled his cereal all over the table. She wanted to yell, but instead, she took a deep breath and helped him clean it up. Later that day, her teacher dropped some papers, and Mia helped her pick them up too.

When Mia got home, her mom said, "You've been such a helper today. You make this house brighter!"

Mia smiled. She realized something — being kind made her feel happy too.

That's how kindness works. When you show love and patience, it doesn't just help others — it fills your own heart with God's light. Kindness always starts with a choice, and that choice begins inside you.

KINDNESS STATRTS WITH YOU

Heart Lesson:
You don't have to wait for someone else to be kind first. You can start it! Kindness is like a spark — when you share it, it spreads everywhere.

Action Challenge:
Think of one person who could use a little kindness this week — maybe someone lonely, shy, or grumpy.

Do one small act for them — a smile, a kind word, or a helping hand — and see how it changes the day.

Prayer:
Dear God, thank You for showing me how to be kind. Help me to start kindness wherever I go and let it grow from my heart to others. Amen.

WEEK 6
THE POWER OF A KIND WORD

Bible Verse:
"Kind words are like honey—sweet to the soul and healthy for the body."
— Proverbs 16:24 (NLT)

Heart Talk:
Have you ever had someone say something nice to you — maybe, "I'm proud of you," or "You're my friend"?

Do you remember how it made you feel?

Kind words can turn a sad day into a happy one. They can make someone who feels invisible feel seen.

But sometimes, we forget how powerful our words are. Words can lift others up — or knock them down. That's why God wants us to use our voices to speak love, truth, and encouragement. When you use kind words, you're sharing a little piece of God's heart with the world.

Even a simple "thank you," "I'm sorry," or "I

love you" can shine light into someone's heart.

THE POWER OF A KIND WORD

Think and Shine

What kind words has someone spoken to you that made you feel special?

What's something kind you can say to a friend, teacher, or family member this week?

How can you use your words to make someone smile today?

Action Challenge:
Write down three kind words or phrases you want to use more often this week — and make it your goal to say them at least once a day!

Example:
"You're doing great!"

"I'm glad you're my friend."

"Thank you for helping me."

Prayer:
Dear God, thank You for giving me words that can bless others. Help me use them wisely — to encourage, comfort, and share Your love everywhere I go. Amen.

WEEK 7

THE FORGIVENESS

Bible Verse:
"Make allowance for each other's faults, and forgive anyone who offends you. Remember, the Lord forgave you, so you must forgive others."
— Colossians 3:13 (NLT)

Reflection:
Forgiveness isn't always easy. Sometimes people hurt our feelings, say unkind things, or forget to include us. It's normal to feel sad or angry — but holding onto those feelings is like carrying a heavy backpack everywhere you go.

When you forgive, it's like taking that backpack off. You feel lighter, freer, and brighter inside. That's what God wants for you — not a heavy heart, but a shining one!

When we forgive others, we're showing the same love God gives to us every single day. Forgiveness doesn't mean what happened was okay — it means you're choosing peace over pain.

Creative Activity: "The Forgiveness Heart"

You'll need:

Paper, scissors, and crayons or markers.

Step 1: Draw a big heart and cut it out.

Step 2: On one side, write or draw things that make your heart feel heavy — like anger, hurt, or someone you need to forgive.

THE FORGIVENESS

Step 3: On the other side, write or draw what your heart feels like when you forgive — peace, love, joy, or light.

Step 4: Pray over your heart and ask God to help you let go of the heavy side and fill your heart with His light.

You can hang it somewhere to remind you that a forgiving heart shines brightest!

Heart Lesson:
Forgiveness doesn't just help others — it helps you. When you let go, your heart glows with God's peace.

Prayer:
Dear God, thank You for forgiving me every day. Help me forgive others, even when it's hard, and fill my heart with Your light and peace. Amen.

WEEK 8
KINDNESS IN ACTION

Bible Verse:
"Let us not grow weary of doing good, for in due season we will reap, if we do not give up." — Galatians 6:9 (ESV)

Reflection:
Kindness isn't just something we talk about — it's something we do!

Every time you help, share, or comfort someone, you're planting seeds of God's love. Some people might not say "thank you," and that's okay — because God sees every kind thing you do.

Sometimes, being kind means doing the right thing even when no one notices. Other times, it means showing love when it's not easy — like forgiving, helping a sibling, or smiling at someone who's been unkind.

Every act of kindness is like a spark that makes the world a little brighter. When we keep doing good, even when it's hard, our light keeps shining for God.

Shine Challenge of the Week: "Project Kindness"
This week, pick one act of kindness to do each day.

KINDNESS IN ACTION

Here are a few ideas to inspire you:
Write a note or draw a picture to encourage someone.

Help at home without being asked.

Sit with someone who looks lonely.

Say something nice about someone behind their back (a good kind of gossip!).

Pray for someone who might need a little extra love.

At the end of the week, think about which act made your heart feel the warmest — that's God's light glowing in you!

Heart Lesson:
Kindness grows stronger when you keep sharing it — and it shines brightest when you do it from the heart.

KINDNESS IN ACTION

Prayer:
Dear God, thank You for showing me how powerful kindness can be. Help me to keep doing good, even when it's hard, and use my actions to show Your love to others. Amen.

A Bright Story from Miss Susan: The Little Act That Made a Big Difference

When I was in school, there was a girl named Grace who always sat by herself. She didn't talk much, and most of the other kids ignored her. One day, during lunch, I felt something inside whisper, "Go sit with her."

At first, I didn't want to. What if she didn't want company? What if my friends thought it was weird?

But the feeling wouldn't go away — so I took my lunch tray, smiled, and sat next to her.

Grace looked surprised, but then she smiled back. We talked about our favorite foods, and I found out she loved drawing and reading — just like me! After that day, we sat together often. A few weeks later, she told me, "I used to feel invisible. But now I feel like I belong."

KINDNESS IN ACTION

Her words stayed in my heart. That one small act — just sitting beside someone — became a friendship that lasted for years. I learned that kindness doesn't have to be big or fancy. Sometimes it's just showing up when someone needs light the most. So, whenever you wonder if your kindness.

really matters, remember this: even one gentle act can change someone's whole day — maybe even their whole heart.

Reflection Question:
Who can you show kindness to this week — someone who might be feeling left out, quiet, or unseen?

WEEK 9
ROOTED IN GOD'S WORD

Bible Verse:
"Your word is a lamp to guide my feet and a light for my path."
— Psalm 119:105 (NLT)

Heart Talk:
Have you ever walked in the dark and needed a flashlight? God's Word is like that light — it helps us see where to step, where to turn, and where to stop.

The Bible isn't just a storybook — it's a life guide from God. Every time we read it, our hearts grow stronger, our faith gets deeper, and our light shines brighter.

When you remember Bible verses or read even a few lines each day, you're planting roots in your heart. Roots help trees stand strong when the wind blows. God's Word helps you stand strong when life feels confusing or hard.

The more you read, the deeper your roots grow — and the more beautiful your faith becomes!

Creative Activity: "Planting God's Word"
You'll need:
A small cup or pot, soil, and a seed (any kind — a bean, sunflower, or even a flower seed).

ROOTED IN GOD'S WORD

1. Fill your cup with soil.
2. Gently plant your seed and water it.
3. On a small card or label, write a Bible verse (like Psalm 119:105) and tape it to your cup.

4. Every time you water your seed, say your verse out loud and thank God for helping your faith grow too.

Watch as your seed sprouts — just like your heart will when you spend time in God's Word!

Think and Shine:
What's one Bible verse that helps you when you're scared, sad, or unsure?
How can reading the Bible make your heart stronger?
Who can you share your favorite verse with this week?

Prayer:
Dear God, thank You for Your Word that lights my path and helps me grow strong.

Teach me to love Your truth and to let it take root deep in my heart.

Help me shine bright with faith and love every day. Amen.

WEEK 10
PATIENCE IN THE WAITING

Bible Verse:
"Be still before the Lord and wait patiently for him."
— Psalm 37:7 (NIV)

Heart Talk:
Waiting can feel so hard!

Maybe you're waiting for a birthday, a new toy, an answer to a prayer, or something you really hope will happen soon.

Sometimes it feels like nothing is happening — but did you know that God is always working, even while we wait?

Think about a flower seed. When it's in the ground, you can't see it growing. But beneath the soil, roots are spreading, life is forming, and something beautiful is getting ready to bloom.

That's how God works in our hearts. He uses waiting to make us stronger, wiser, and more trusting. When we're patient, we're telling God, "I trust You. I believe You know what's best."

PATIENCE IN THE WAITING

Even when it feels quiet or slow, God's timing is always perfect.

Creative Activity: "The Patience Flower"
 You'll need:
  Paper, scissors, and crayons or colored pencils.

1. Draw a big flower with several petals.

2. On each petal, write or draw something you're waiting for — like a prayer, a dream, or a hope.

3. In the center of the flower, write "God's Perfect Time."

Decorate your flower and hang it somewhere you'll see it often.

Every time you look at your Patience Flower, take a deep breath and whisper:
"God is working, even while I wait."

PATIENCE IN THE WAITING

Think and Shine:

What's something you're waiting for right now?

How can you use this waiting time to grow closer to God?

How do you feel when you remember that God's timing is always right?

Prayer:

Dear God, sometimes it's hard to wait.

Please help me to be patient and to trust that You are working, even when I can't see it.

Teach me to rest in Your love and believe in Your perfect timing. Amen.

WEEK 11
GROWING THROUGH CHALLENGES

Bible Verse:
"I can do all things through Christ who strengthens me."
— Philippians 4:13 (NKJV)

Heart Talk:
Have you ever faced something that felt really hard — like a big test, learning something new, or a time when you felt left out or disappointed?

It's easy to wonder, "Where is God in this?"

But the truth is — He's right there with you, helping you grow stronger through it.

Think about how a tree grows taller after the rain and wind. The wind may seem rough, but it helps the tree's roots grow deeper and its trunk grow stronger. The same happens with us.

When life feels tough, God is using it to make our hearts brave, kind, and full of faith.

Every challenge you face is an invitation to lean on God's strength — not your own. And when you do, you'll discover that you can stand tall, no matter what storms come your way.

GROWING THROUGH CHALLENGES

Creative Activity: "My Strong Heart Journal"

You'll need:
A notebook or some paper and a pencil.

Write or draw about a time something felt really hard for you. Then, answer these three prompts:

What made it hard?

How did you feel at first?

How did God help you through it (or how can you ask Him to help now)?

When you finish, write this at the bottom of your page:

"God is helping my heart grow strong."

Keep your Strong Heart Journal close — it's your reminder that even through tough days, you're growing in God's love.

GROWING THROUGH CHALLENGES

Think and Shine:

What's something hard you faced that made you stronger?

How can you ask God for strength when things feel too big?

Who can you encourage this week by sharing your story?

Prayer:

Dear God, thank You for being with me when things feel hard.

Please help me remember that challenges help me grow stronger in You.

Give me courage, faith, and a heart that never gives up.

In Jesus' name, Amen.

WEEK 12
GRATEFUL HEARTS GROW BRIGHT

Bible Verse:
"Give thanks in all circumstances; for this is God's will for you in Christ Jesus." — 1 Thessalonians 5:18 (NIV)

Heart Talk:
Have you noticed how sunshine makes flowers open wide?

That's what thankfulness does to our hearts — it helps us open up to God's goodness.

Sometimes we focus on what we don't have or what's not going right. But when we start to thank God for what we do have — even the small things — our hearts begin to shine.

Being thankful doesn't mean everything is perfect. It means we trust that God is working in every season — in the sunny days and the rainy ones. When we practice gratitude, we grow stronger, happier, and more content. A grateful heart is like good soil — it helps God's love take root and bloom beautifully inside us.

GRATEFUL HEARTS GROW BRIGHT

Creative Activity: "The Thankful Garden"
You'll need:
Paper, crayons or markers, and scissors.

1. Draw a big garden with flowers, trees, or anything you like.

2. On each flower petal, write or draw something you're thankful for — like family, Friends, school, your favorite food, or even your smile!

3. Around the garden, write this verse: "Give thanks in all circumstances."

4. Each day this week, add a new flower to your garden as you think of more blessings.

Soon, you'll have a garden full of gratitude!

Think and Shine:
What are three things you're thankful for today?

How can being thankful change the way you see your day?

Who can you say "thank you" to this week — and really mean it?

Prayer:
Dear God, thank You for all the blessings You give me — big and small. Help me to see the good in every day and to grow with a grateful heart. When I start to complain, remind me of all the ways You love and care for me. Amen.

GRATEFUL HEARTS GROW BRIGHT

A Bright Story With Miss Susan: My Rainy Day Reminder

One weekend, it rained nonstop. The sky was gray, my plans got canceled, and I felt a little grumpy. I had planned to go to the park with my niece, but instead, we were stuck inside.

She looked out the window and said, "Auntie Susan, it's too rainy to play!"

I nodded and sighed, "Yes, sweetie, it's not the day I hoped for."

A few minutes later, she came running back with her rain boots on, holding an umbrella almost bigger than she was. She said, "Let's thank God for the puddles!"

I couldn't help but laugh — her joy was contagious!

So, we went outside, jumping in puddles, splashing, and laughing until our sides hurt.

By the time we came back in, we were soaked — but smiling from ear to ear.

GRATEFUL HEARTS GROW BRIGHT

That night, as I dried our shoes by the door,
I whispered a little prayer:

"Thank You, Lord, for turning my rainy day into a thankful one."

I realized gratitude doesn't wait for everything to go right — it looks for the light in every moment.
Sometimes, all it takes is a child's joy to remind us that even rainy days can shine.

Think and Shine:

Have you ever had a day that didn't go as planned?
What's something good that came out of it anyway?

Prayer:
Dear God, thank You for teaching me to be thankful in every moment — sunny or rainy.

Help me to see the joy You hide in ordinary days and keep my heart bright with gratitude.
Amen.

WEEK 13
FILLED WITH GOD'S LOVE

Bible Verse:
"We love because He first loved us."

— 1 John 4:19 (NIV)

Heart Talk:

Have you ever tried to pour water from an empty cup? You can't — because there's nothing inside!

Our hearts are a little like that cup. When we're filled with God's love, it overflows — and we can share it with others.

But when we forget how much God loves us, it's easy to feel tired, sad, or even mean.

That's why it's so important to spend time with God — reading His Word, singing songs, or just talking to Him. Each time we do, He fills our hearts again with His love, peace, and joy.

Then, when someone needs a smile, a hug, or a helping hand — we'll have plenty of love to give!

This week, remember: you are deeply loved by God.
Let His love fill you up until it overflows to everyone around you.

FILLED WITH GOD'S LOVE

Creative Activity: "Love Overflows Cup"
You'll need:
   Paper, crayons or markers, scissors.
1. Draw a big cup or heart in the center of your page.
2. Inside it, write or draw things that show God's love — like family, friends, forgiveness, or Jesus' cross.
3. Around the cup, draw love "overflowing" — hearts, smiles, or kind actions you can do for others.
4. Hang your drawing where you'll see it every morning to remind yourself: "I'm filled with God's love!"

Think and Shine:
   What fills your heart with love and joy?
   How can you share that love with someone this week?

Prayer:
Dear God, thank You for loving me first.
Fill my heart with Your love until it overflows.
Help me to share that love through my words and actions every day.
Amen.

WEEK 14
THE POWER OF A LOVING HEART

Bible Verse:
"Let all that you do be done in love."

— 1 Corinthians 16:14 (ESV)

Heart Talk:

Have you ever noticed how one smile can make someone's whole day better?

That's what happens when love is in your heart — it spreads light wherever you go!

Sometimes, we think love has to be big — like giving gifts or doing something amazing. But most of the time, love shows up in small ways:

Listening when someone talks
Helping your parents without being asked
Saying kind words when it's hard
Forgiving when you'd rather stay upset
When we do these things, we are walking in God's love.

God's love doesn't just stay inside us — it moves through us. It makes the

THE POWER OF A LOVING HEART

world softer, kinder, and brighter.

This week, remember: your loving heart has power!

Every gentle word, every kind act, every patient choice makes God's light shine a little brighter through you.

Creative Activity: **"Love Lights"**

You'll need:
Paper, scissors, crayons or markers.
1. Draw little hearts and cut them out.
2. On each heart, write one way you can show love this week (like "help Mom," "be kind to my friend," "pray for someone").
Tape the hearts to your bedroom door or mirror.
3. Each time you do one, color it in — and watch your "Love Lights" glow brighter each day!

THE POWER OF A LOVING HEART

Think and Shine:

What's one small way you can show love at home or school today?

How does it feel when someone shows love to you?

Prayer:

Dear Jesus, thank You for filling my heart with Your love.

Help me to share it in big and small ways — with smiles, words, and kind actions.

Let my heart shine bright with love every day.

Amen.

WEEK 15
FORGIVE AND SHINE

Bible Verse:
"Be kind and compassionate to one another, forgiving each other, just as in Christ God forgave you." — Ephesians 4:32 (NIV)

Heart Talk:

Sometimes people hurt our feelings. Maybe a friend said something unkind or someone forgot to include you. It hurts — and that's okay to admit.

But here's something beautiful: when we forgive, it's like opening a window and letting God's light back into our hearts.

Holding on to anger or hurt can make our hearts feel heavy, but forgiveness sets us free.

Forgiving doesn't mean saying what happened was okay — it means giving the pain to God and choosing peace instead.

That's what Jesus did for us. He forgave even when it was hard, showing us how love can heal anything.

FORGIVE AND SHINE

When you choose to forgive, you let your heart shine brighter — because nothing blocks God's light anymore.

Creative Activity: "Let It Go Balloons"

You'll need:

Paper, crayons or markers, scissors.

1. Draw 3–5 balloons on paper.
2. Inside each balloon, write or draw something you want to forgive — maybe a hurt feeling, a mistake, or a time you were upset.
3. Pray and say, "God, I let this go. Help me forgive."
4. Then draw the balloons floating up into the sky — a sign that you've released those feelings to God.

Think and Shine:

What happens to your heart when you hold onto hurt?
How does it feel when you finally forgive?

Prayer:

Dear Jesus, thank You for forgiving me and loving me always.
Help me to forgive others, even when it's hard.
Fill my heart with peace and light so I can shine for You.
Amen.

WEEK 16
LOVING THE UNLOVABLE

Bible Verse:
"But I tell you, love your enemies and pray for those who persecute you."
— Matthew 5:44 (NIV)

Heart Talk:
Some people are easy to love — like your best friend, your grandma, or your pet who always makes you smile.

But what about the person who teases you? Or the classmate who never wants to share?

It's not easy to be kind when others aren't kind to us.

But Jesus teaches us something amazing — we can still love them.

When we love someone who isn't acting lovable, we show them what God's heart looks like.

Maybe they're having a bad day. Maybe they don't know how much God loves them yet.

Your kindness could be the very thing that helps them see God's light for the first time!

LOVING THE UNLOVABLE

You don't have to be best friends with everyone, but you can choose to be gentle, forgiving, and kind — because love is stronger than meanness, stronger than anger, and stronger than hate.

Creative Activity: "Kindness Chain"
You'll need:
Strips of paper, crayons or markers, glue or tape.
1. Cut paper into strips.
2. On each strip, write one loving action you can do — even for someone hard to love. (Example: "Say something nice," "Share a toy," "Pray for them.")
3. Loop the strips together to make a paper chain.
4. Hang it where you can see it all week — your Kindness Chain will remind you that every act of love makes the world brighter!

Think and Shine:
Who is someone that's hard for you to love right now?
What's one kind thing you could do for them this week?

Prayer:
Dear Jesus,
Thank You for loving everyone — even when we make mistakes.
Help me love others the same way You love me.
Teach me to be kind, patient, and forgiving, even when it's hard.
Let Your light shine through me every day.
Amen

WEEK 17
SHINE THROUGH HELPING HANDS

Bible Verse:
"Serve one another humbly in love."
— Galatians 5:13 (NIV)

Heart Talk:
Do you know what makes your hands extra special?
God made them to help others!
When you tie your friend's shoe, help your mom set the table, or pick up toys without being asked — that's love in action.

Love isn't just a word we say. It's something we do.

Jesus showed love with His hands — healing, helping, comforting, and even washing His friends' feet.
(Imagine that — the Son of God doing something so humble!)Noted

When you use your hands to help, your heart grows softer and brighter.

You're showing people that God's love is alive and real — right through you.

This week, let's make our hands "helping hands" that shine with love!

SHINE THROUGH HELPING HANDS

Creative Activity: "Helping Hands Poster"

You'll need:

Paper, crayons or markers, scissors.

Trace both your hands on paper and cut them out.

On each hand, write one way you can help someone this week — like "help Mom cook," "clean up toys," or "be kind to my teacher."

Decorate your hands with bright colors and tape them somewhere you'll see them every day.

Each time you help, you're letting your light shine!

Think and Shine:

What's one way your hands can show love today?

How does helping someone make you feel inside?

Prayer:

Dear Jesus,

Thank You for giving me hands that can help and a heart that can love.

Show me ways to serve others with kindness and joy.

Let my helping hands shine Your light everywhere I go.

Amen.

WEEK 18

SPEAK LOVE EVERYWHERE YOU GO

Bible Verse:
"Let your conversation be always full of grace."
— Colossians 4:6 (NIV)

Heart Talk:

Your words are like little seeds, and everywhere you go, you plant them — at home, in school, on the playground.

When you plant kind words, they grow into smiles, friendship, and joy.

But when we speak unkind words, they can make hearts feel sad or small.

That's why God asks us to speak with grace — that means to use words that are gentle, caring, and full of love.

Even a simple "Good job," "You can do it," or "I forgive you" can turn someone's day around.

The more we practice speaking love, the more it becomes our natural way of talking — just like Jesus.

SPEAK LOVE EVERYWHERE YOU GO

He used His words to lift people up, not tear them down. And when we do the same, we shine His light with every sentence we say.

Creative Activity: **"Love Words Cloud"**

You'll need:

Paper, crayons or markers, scissors.

1. Cut your paper into the shape of a big fluffy cloud.
2. Inside the cloud, write or draw all the loving words you can think of — like "kind," "thank you," "I love you," "you're special," "Jesus loves you."
3. Decorate it with sunshine rays and hang it where everyone can see.
4. Each time you look at it, remember: your words can bring light wherever you go!

Think and Shine:

What are some words that make you feel loved?

How can your words show God's love to others this week?

Prayer:

Dear Jesus,

Thank You for teaching me to use my words for love.

Help me speak kindly and gently — even when I feel upset.

Let my words be like sunshine, bringing warmth and joy to others.

Amen.

WEEK 19
LOVE THAT LISTENS

Bible Verse:
"Everyone should be quick to listen, slow to speak and slow to become angry." — James 1:19 (NIV)

Heart Talk:
Have you ever felt really happy when someone listened to you — like they cared about every word you said?

That's the power of listening love.

When we stop talking, look someone in the eyes, and really listen, we're showing them they matter.

Jesus was a great listener.

He didn't rush people or talk over them — He cared about what they were feeling and thinking.

That's how people knew they were loved.

Sometimes listening means being quiet when you want to speak.

Other times, it means showing patience, even when someone takes a long time to finish.

LOVE THAT LISTENS

Every time you listen with kindness, your heart becomes a mirror of God's love.

So this week, let's practice listening not just with our ears — but with our hearts!

Creative Activity: **"Listening Ears Craft" You'll need:**
Paper, crayons, scissors, glue or tape.

1. Draw two big ears on paper and cut them out.

2. Decorate them with bright colors and write these words: "I listen with love."

3. Tape them to a headband or a strip of paper to wear like a crown.

4. When you wear your "listening ears," remember — love starts with paying attention!

Think and Shine:
How do you feel when someone listens carefully to you?

Who can you show love to this week by really listening?

Prayer:
Dear Jesus,

Thank You for always hearing me when I pray.

Teach me to listen with love — not just with my ears, but with my heart. Help me be patient and kind when others are speaking.

Amen.

WEEK 20
WHEN GOD IS QUIET

Bible Verse:
"Be still before the lord and wait patiently for him"
— Psalm 37:7(NIV)

Heart Talk:
There are moments in our faith journey when God feels quiet. We pray, we listen, we wait—and yet, nothing seems to happen. No clear answers. No sudden change. Just silence.

But God's silence does not mean His absence.

Sometimes, God is doing His deepest work when He is the quietest. In those still moments, He is shaping our character, strengthening our trust, and teaching us how to lean on Him rather than on quick answers.

Being still is not easy. It requires patience and surrender. It asks us to trust God even when we don't understand His timing. Yet it is often in the waiting that our faith grows roots—strong, steady, and unshakable.

When God is quiet, He is inviting us closer. He is asking us to slow down, listen with our hearts, and trust that He is working behind the scenes. What feels like a pause may actually be preparation.

WHEN GOD IS QUIET

Reflect and Shine:
Have you ever felt like God was quiet in your life?

What might God be teaching you during this season of waiting?

How can you practice stillness and trust this week?

Quiet Practice: "Stillness Space"
Find a quiet place and sit for one minute each day this week.
Take slow breaths and repeat this prayer in your heart: "Lord, i trust You."
Let the quiet become a place of peace instead of worry.

Prayer:
Dear God,
When You feel quiet, help me remember that You are still near.

Teach me to trust You in the waiting and to rest in Your presence.

Strengthen my faith when answers don't come quickly, and help me believe that You are always working for my good. Amen.

WHEN GOD IS QUIET

A Bright Story with Miss Susan — "The Last Cookie"

One afternoon, my daughter and I baked a batch of cookies together. The house smelled so sweet!

When we finished, there was just one cookie left on the plate. I smiled and said, "Go ahead, sweetheart, you can have it." But she shook her head and said, "No, Mommy, let's give it to Grandma. She loves cookies."

My heart melted.

In that little moment, i saw God's love shining right through her — simple, thoughtful, and pure. Love doesn't wait to be asked. It just gives.

Think and Shine:

What's one small thing you can give or share this week to show love?

WEEK 21
JOYS COMES FROM JESUS

Bible Verse:

"The joy of the Lord is your strength."

— Nehemiah 8:10 (NIV)

Heart Talk:

Have you ever had a day when nothing seemed to go right — maybe you dropped your ice cream, forgot your homework, or got caught in the rain?

Those moments can make us frown, but here's something amazing: joy doesn't come from what happens around us — it comes from Who lives inside us!

When Jesus lives in your heart, He gives you a joy that doesn't fade — not even on a tough day.

You can smile through the rain, laugh in the middle of mistakes, and find peace when things feel hard, because His love never leaves you.

Joy is like sunshine that starts on the inside and shines out for everyone to see!

JOYS COMES FROM JESUS

Creative Activity: **"Joy Jar"**

You'll need:

A jar, paper, crayons, or markers.

1. Decorate your jar with the words "My Joy Jar."
2. Each day this week, write or draw one thing that made you smile.
3. At the end of the week, open the jar and thank God for every joyful moment!

Even small joys — like a hug, a rainbow, or your favorite song — are gifts from God!

Think and Shine:

What makes you smile even on hard days?

How can you spread joy to someone else this week?

Prayer:

Dear Jesus,

Thank You for filling my heart with Your joy.

Even when things go wrong, help me to smile and trust You.

Let my joy shine so others can see Your love in me.

Amen.

JOYS COMES FROM JESUS

Bible Verse:

"This is the day that the Lord has made; let us rejoice and be glad in it."

— Psalm 118:24 (NIV)

Heart Talk:

Every morning, we get to make a choice — to smile or to frown, to grumble or to give thanks.

Joy doesn't wait for everything to be perfect. Joy says, "I'll be happy because God made today!"

Some days, things might not go as planned — maybe your friend doesn't share, or you lose a game.

But choosing joy means saying, "God is still good, and I can still be thankful."

Joy isn't pretending to be happy; it's trusting that God is with you, even in the little disappointments.

JOYS COMES FROM JESUS

When you choose joy, you light up your day — and you might just brighten someone else's, too.

Creative Activity: **"Joyful Morning Mirror"**
You'll need:
 A small mirror or a piece of paper and markers.
1. Write this on your mirror (or paper):
    "God made this day — I will rejoice!"
2. Each morning, look in the mirror, smile, and say it out loud!
3. Then, think of one thing you're thankful for and one way you can spread joy today.

Watch how your whole day feels different when you start with joy!
 Think and Shine:
 What helps you choose joy when you don't feel happy?
 How can your smile or attitude help someone else find joy?

Prayer:
Dear God,
Thank You for today!
Even when things are hard, help me choose joy.
Let my smile remind others that You made this day and You are good.
Amen.

WEEK 22
DON'T LET ANYONE STEAL YOUR JOY

Bible Verse:
"Always be full of joy in the Lord. I say it again—rejoice!"
— Philippians 4:4 (NLT)

Heart Talk: Have you ever been in a good mood — maybe humming a song, smiling big — and then someone says something mean or you get in trouble, and poof! your joy disappears?

It happens to everyone sometimes! But God wants us to remember: our joy doesn't come from what people say or do — it comes from Him.

That means no one can take it away unless we let them.

Even when others are grumpy or things don't go our way, we can keep our joy by choosing to stay peaceful and thankful.

Joy is like a light inside your heart. Don't let anyone blow it out — protect it, keep it shining, and let it remind you that God is always with you.

Creative Activity: **"Joy Shield"** You'll need:
Paper, crayons or markers, and scissors.
1. Draw a big shield on your paper.
2. Inside the shield, write things that help protect your joy — like prayer, music, reading the Bible, being thankful, kindness, and forgiveness.

DON'T LET ANYONE STEAL YOUR JOY

3. Around the shield, draw things that try to steal your joy — like anger, jealousy, or fear. Hang your Joy Shield where you can see it as a reminder that your joy comes from God!

Think and Shine:
What makes your joy feel strong?
What can you do when someone tries to make you feel upset or sad?

Prayer:
Dear God, Thank You for giving me joy that no one can take away.
When things are hard or people aren't kind, help me protect my joy.
Let my smile show others that You live in my heart.
Amen.

WEEK 23

JOY THROUGH PRAISE

Bible Verse:
"Let everything that has breath praise the Lord."
— Psalm 150:6 (NIV)

Heart Talk: Do you ever sing your favorite song at the top of your lungs?

When you sing to God, it's like your heart is smiling!

Praise isn't just singing — it's a way of saying, "Thank You, God, for who You are!"

We can praise Him when we're happy and when we're sad, because praising reminds us that God is always good and always near.

Even when things don't go our way, praising God can turn our worries into joy. It's like turning on a light in a dark room — praise helps our hearts shine bright again!

When we praise God, He fills us with peace, strength, and happiness that never fades.

JOY THROUGH PRAISE

Creative Activity: "Praise Parade!"
You'll need:
Music, paper, crayons, and your best dance moves!
1. Choose a joyful song that praises God.
2. Draw colorful flags or banners with words like JOY, THANK YOU, GOD, or PRAISE!
3. Have your own "Praise Parade" at home or in Sunday school — sing, dance, and celebrate all that God has done!
4. End by thanking Him for filling your heart with joy.

Think and Shine:
What are some ways you can praise God besides singing?
How does praising God make you feel inside?

Prayer:
Dear God,
Thank You for giving me songs of joy and praise.
When I sing and thank You, I feel Your love all around me.
Help me to praise You every day — with my words, my heart, and my smile!
Amen.

WEEK 24

LET YOUR JOY SHINE

Bible Verse: "You are the light of the world—like a city on a hill that cannot be hidden."
— Matthew 5:14 (NLT)

Heart Talk: Have you ever seen how one candle can light another?

Even a small flame can fill a dark room with light.

That's what joy does! When you let God's joy shine in you — through your smile, your laughter, your kindness — it spreads to everyone around you.

Joy is contagious! When you choose to stay positive, grateful, and loving, you help others see God's light, too.

It's not always easy, but even a small act — like cheering someone up or saying something kind — can turn a gloomy day into a bright one.

Let your joy be the spark that lights up your world!

Creative Activity: "Joy Sparks"
You'll need:
Paper stars, scissors, and crayons or markers.

1. Cut out several star shapes.

LET YOUR JOY SHINE

2. On each star, write one way you can share joy this week (like "help my friend," "say thank you," or "smile at someone").
3. Decorate them with bright colors and hang them where you can see them — maybe on your wall or a window!

Every time you do one, thank God for helping your joy shine.

Think and Shine:
Who needs a little extra joy this week?
What can you do to brighten someone's day?

Prayer:
Dear Jesus,
Thank You for filling my heart with joy. Help me to let that joy shine wherever I go — at school, at home, and with my friends.

Make me a light that shows Your love to everyone around me.

Amen.

LET YOUR JOY SHINE

A Bright Story with Miss Susan — "The Morning Mix-Up"

One busy morning, I woke up late. The alarm hadn't gone off, and everything felt rushed — breakfast wasn't ready, and I couldn't find my keys. I felt flustered and almost said, "This day is ruined!"

But I stopped for a moment, took a deep breath, and whispered, "God, please help me find peace even when things don't go right."

I slowed down just a little. I made some toast, found my keys under a pile of books, and smiled to myself.

By the time I stepped outside, the sun was shining and the air was fresh. I felt calm — not because everything was perfect, but because I had invited God into my morning.

Sometimes peace isn't in the quiet moments — it's in the choice to stay calm when everything feels loud.

Think and Shine:

When your day starts off rough, what can you do to find peace?

How can you invite God into your morning?

WEEK 25

BE STILL AND FEEL GOD'S PEACE

Bible Verse:

"Be still, and know that I am God."

— Psalm 46:10 (NIV)

Heart Talk:

Have you ever tried to sit very still — no talking, no moving — just quiet?

It's not easy! Sometimes our minds are full of thoughts and our hearts feel busy.

But God whispers to us, "Be still."

That means we don't have to fix everything or rush everywhere. We can stop, take a breath, and remember that God is in control.

When we take time to be still — even for a minute — we make room for God's peace to fill us.

It's like sitting beside a calm lake after a long day. The water is quiet… and so is your heart.

God's peace isn't loud or flashy — it's soft, gentle, and always there when we slow down enough to feel it.

BE STILL AND FEEL GOD'S PEACE

Creative Activity: **"Peace Bubbles"**
You'll need:

A cup of bubble mix and a wand (or make your own with dish soap and water).

1. Go outside on a calm day.
2. Blow bubbles slowly and watch them float away.
3. As you blow, whisper one worry to God and let it drift off with each bubble.

Watch how light and free you feel when you let go — that's what God's peace feels like!

Think and Shine:

When do you feel peaceful?

What helps you be still and remember that God is near?

WEEK 26
BE A PEACEMAKER

Bible Verse:
"Blessed are the peacemakers, for they will be called children of God."
— Matthew 5:9 (NIV)

Heart Talk:

Have you ever seen two friends argue? Maybe someone grabbed a toy or said something unkind. It can make the room feel heavy, right?

But when someone steps in with kindness, forgiveness, or a calm word — everything begins to feel lighter again.

That's what being a peacemaker means. It doesn't mean pretending everything's okay. It means choosing gentle words instead of angry ones, and forgiveness instead of fighting.

When you help others get along, you're showing God's heart.

You're reminding the world that peace isn't just something we feel — it's something we share. Jesus called peacemakers His children because they act like Him — loving, patient, and full of light.

BE A PEACEMAKER

Creative Activity: "Peace Chain"
You'll need:
Colored paper, scissors, tape or glue, and markers.
1. Cut the paper into strips.
2. On each strip, write one peaceful thing you can do —
   like "say sorry," "share," "pray," "help a friend," or "give a hug."
3. Link them together to make a long Peace Chain.

Think and Shine:
When have you helped make peace between friends or family?

What's one way you can show God's peace this week?

Prayer:

Dear God,
Thank You for filling my heart with Your peace.

Help me to use kind words, gentle hands, and a loving heart.

Show me how to bring peace wherever I go — at home, at school, and with my friends.

Let Your light shine through me today.

Amen.

WEEK 27
TRUSTING GOD STEP BY STEP

Bible Verse:
"Trust in the Lord with all your heart and lean not on your own understanding; in all your ways submit to Him, and He will make your paths straight."
— Proverbs 3:5–6 (NIV)

Heart Talk:

Have you ever walked through a dark room and had to take small steps carefully because you couldn't see everything ahead?

That's what trusting God is like sometimes. We can't always see the whole plan — but God does. He sees the path, the turns, and the bright ending waiting for us.

When we choose to trust Him, even when things don't make sense, we're showing faith.

Faith says, "God, I can't see everything, but I know You can — and that's enough.

"Each time we take a step of trust — by praying, obeying, or being patient — our hearts grow stronger.

Little by little, our faith gets brighter, just like a candle that never goes out.

TRUSTING GOD STEP BY STEP

Creative Activity: "Faith Footprints"
You'll need:
Paper, crayons or paint, and scissors.
1. Trace or paint your footprints on paper.
2. Inside each footprint, write one way you can show trust this week — like pray before worrying, be patient, or thank God even when waiting.
3. Tape them in a line to make your "Faith Path." Each time you walk past, remember: you're walking in trust, one step at a time.

Think and Shine: What's something you've had to trust God for recently? How does trusting God make you feel inside?

Prayer:
Dear God,
Thank You for knowing the way, even when I can't see it.

Help me to trust You with my whole heart. When I feel unsure, remind me that You are leading me one step at a time.

I know Your plans are good, and I choose to follow You.

Amen.

WEEK 28

FAITH WHILE YOU WAIT

Bible Verse:
"Be still before the Lord and wait patiently for Him."
— Psalm 37:7 (NIV)

Heart Talk:

Waiting is hard!

Maybe you've waited for your birthday, a special trip, or an answer to a prayer.

Waiting can feel like forever! But do you know what's special about waiting with faith?

It means we believe God is working, even when we can't see it yet.

Sometimes God says "yes," sometimes "no," and sometimes "wait."

That "wait" is not a "no" — it's God preparing something good in the right time.

When we keep praying, stay thankful, and trust His heart, our faith grows stronger.

It's like planting a seed — you can't see the roots growing under the soil, but something beautiful is happening.

So when you're waiting, don't give up.

FAITH WHILE YOU WAIT

Keep trusting, keep shining, and know that God is never late — He's always right on time.

Creative Activity: "Faith Flower"
You'll need:
Paper, crayons, scissors, and glue.
1. Draw and cut out a flower with petals.
2. On each petal, write something you're waiting for or praying about.
3. In the center, write "I trust God."
4. Each time you pray and choose to wait with faith, color in a petal.

Soon, your flower will be full — just like your faith!

Think and Shine:
What is something you're waiting for right now?

How can you show faith while you wait?

Prayer: Dear God,
Thank You for always working for my good — even when I can't see it yet.
Help me to be patient and trust Your perfect timing.
When I start to feel tired of waiting, remind me that You never forget me.
I will keep believing, because You are faithful.
Amen.

WEEK 29
WHEN PLANS CHANGE

Bible Verse:
"We can make our plans, but the Lord determines our steps."
— Proverbs 16:9 (NLT)

Heart Talk:

Have you ever been excited about a plan — maybe a picnic, a trip, or a playdate — and then it got canceled?

It's hard when things don't go the way we hoped.

But here's something amazing: even when our plans change, God's plan never fails.

Sometimes He changes our direction to protect us, to help us grow, or to lead us somewhere even better.

We may not understand it right away, but we can trust that He always knows what's best.

When we let go of "my way" and say, "God, I trust Your way," peace fills our hearts again.

That's what faith looks like — believing that God is good, 71 71 even when the day doesn't go how we wanted.

WHEN PLANS CHANGE

Creative Activity: "God's Better Plan" Puzzle
You'll need:
Paper, scissors, and crayons.
1. Draw a big heart and decorate it.
2. Cut it into puzzle pieces.
3. On each piece, write something that didn't go your way — like rained out picnic, lost toy, or changed plans.
4. As you put the heart back together, say: "Even when I don't understand, God's plan fits together perfectly."

Think and Shine:
When was a time your plans changed but turned out okay?

How can you remember to trust God when things don't go as you hoped?

Prayer:
Dear God,
Thank You that Your plans are always good.
When my plans change, help me to stay calm and trust You.
Teach me to see the good You are doing, even when I don't understand.
I know You are guiding every step I take.
Amen.

WHEN PLANS CHANGE

A Bright Story with Miss Susan — **"The Ice Cream Detour"**

One sunny afternoon, I planned to run a few errands — get groceries, mail a package, and hurry home.

But on the way, I got stuck in traffic. Cars weren't moving, and my list would have to wait.

So, instead of getting frustrated, I turned down a side street and stopped at a little ice cream shop I'd never noticed before.

Inside, I met a tired mom with her two kids.

We started talking, and before long, we were laughing and sharing stories about God's goodness.

As I left, the mom smiled and said, "I really needed that today."

Driving home, I realized — maybe God wanted that meeting to happen more than my errands.

Sometimes, when plans change, it's because He's guiding us toward a sweeter moment.

WEEK 30
WHEN I FEEL WEAK, GOD IS STRENGHT

Bible Verse:
"My grace is all you need. My power works best in weakness."
— 2 Corinthians 12:9 (NLT)

Heart Talk:

Have you ever had a day when everything felt too hard?

Maybe you couldn't figure out your homework, or you dropped the ball at practice, or you just felt tired and grumpy.

We all have those days.

But here's something amazing — when we feel weak, God's strength shines the brightest.

It's like a night sky full of stars — the darker it gets, the brighter they shine.

When we say, "God, I can't do this on my own," He whispers back, "That's okay, I can help you."

You don't have to be the strongest or the fastest. You just have to trust that God is with you — helping, guiding, and lifting you up every single step.

WHEN I FEEL WEAK, GOD IS STRENGHT

Creative Activity: "**God's Helping Hands**"
You'll need:
Paper, pencil, crayons or markers.

1. Trace your hands on the paper.
2. Inside one hand, write or draw things that make you feel weak or worried.
3. Inside the other hand, write or draw how God helps you — like "He comforts me," "He gives me courage," "He loves me."

Hang your picture to remind yourself that your hands — and your heart — are always in God's hands.

Think and Shine:

When do you feel weak or unsure?

How does God help you in those moments?

How can you remind someone else that God is strong for them too?

Prayer:
Dear God,
Thank You for being strong when I feel weak.
Help me remember that Your power works best in my weakness.
Fill my heart with courage and peace every day.
Amen.

WEEK 31
SHINE WITH COURAGE

Bible Verse:
"When I am afraid, I put my trust in You."

— Psalm 56:3 (NIV)

Heart Talk: Sometimes life feels a little scary — a loud thunderstorm, a big test, or trying something new.

But even when our hearts beat fast, we can whisper, "God, I trust You."

Courage isn't about being the biggest or the strongest.

It's about remembering that God is always by your side.

When you trust Him, you can take small steps — one at a time — and shine with quiet bravery.

Just like David faced Goliath with a slingshot and faith, you can face your fears with God's love and strength.

Creative Activity: **"The Courage Cloud"**
You'll need:
Paper, scissors, crayons or markers.

SHINE WITH COURAGE

1. Cut out a big fluffy cloud shape.
2. Inside it, write or draw things that make you afraid.
3. Around the cloud, draw sunbeams and write how God helps you — like "He gives me peace," "He stays with me," "He makes me strong."

Hang your Courage Cloud near your bed to remind you that God's light always breaks through fear.

Think and Shine:
What's something you used to be afraid of that doesn't scare you anymore? How does trusting God make you feel brave?

Who can you help feel braver this week?

Prayer:
Dear God,
Thank You for being my courage when I feel afraid.
Help me remember that You are stronger than my fears.
Fill my heart with peace and bravery so I can shine bright for You.
Amen.

WEEK 32
STANDING STRONG IN FAITH

Bible Verse:

"When I am afraid, I put my trust in You."

— Psalm 56:3 (NIV)

Heart Talk: Sometimes life feels a little scary — a loud thunderstorm, a big test, or trying something new.

But even when our hearts beat fast, we can whisper, "God, I trust You."

Courage isn't about being the biggest or the strongest.

It's about remembering that God is always by your side.

When you trust Him, you can take small steps — one at a time — and shine with quiet bravery.

Just like David faced Goliath with a slingshot and faith, you can face your fears with God's love and strength.

Creative Activity: **"The Courage Cloud"**
You'll need:
   Paper, scissors, crayons or markers.
1. Cut out a big fluffy cloud shape.
2. Inside it, write or draw things that make you afraid.

STANDING STRONG IN FAITH

3. Around the cloud, draw sunbeams and write how God helps you — like "He gives me peace," "He stays with me," "He makes me strong."

Hang your Courage Cloud near your bed to remind you that God's light always breaks through fear.

Think and Shine:

What's something you used to be afraid of that doesn't scare you anymore How does trusting God make you feel brave?

Who can you help feel braver this week?

Prayer:

Dear God,
Thank You for being my courage when I feel afraid.

Help me remember that You are stronger than my fears.

Fill my heart with peace and bravery so I can shine bright for You.

Amen

WEEK 33

SAY WHAT YOU BELIEVE

Bible Verse:
"I believed, and so I spoke."

— 2 Corinthians 4:13 (NIV)

Heart Talk:
When you believe something, it shows in what you say.

If you believe God loves you, you'll say things like,
"God will help me,"
"I can do it," "Everything will be okay."
Those are faith words!

But when we say, "I can't," or "This is too hard," we stop believing what God says about us.

Faith words don't just make us feel better — they remind our hearts that God's promises are true!

When you speak faith, you are telling your worries, "God is bigger!"

So this week, try to let your mouth and your heart agree with God's truth — and watch how your light grows stronger!

SAY WHAT YOU BELIEVE

Creative Activity: "Faith Mirror"
You'll need:
A small mirror, sticky notes, and markers.

1. Write short faith phrases on sticky notes — like "God loves me," "I'm brave," or "I can do hard things."
2. Stick them around your mirror.
3. Every morning, look in the mirror and say one out loud!

It may feel funny at first — but you'll be speaking light into your day.

Think and Shine:

What are some faith words you can say when you feel afraid or unsure?

How do you feel after speaking words that agree with God's promises?

Who can you encourage with faith words this week?

Prayer:
Dear God,
Thank You for giving me faith that speaks.
Help me say what I believe and believe what You say.
Let my words shine with hope and joy every day.
Amen.

WEEK 34
JOY IN THE JOURNEY

Bible Verse:
"You make known to me the path of life; in Your presence there is fullness of joy." — Psalm 16:11 (ESV)

Heart Talk:
Have you ever gone on a trip and asked, "Are we there yet?" Sometimes we're so focused on getting to the end that we forget to enjoy the ride.

But God wants us to find joy right where we are — in each little moment along the way.

Joy can show up in simple things: a bird singing, a hug from someone you love, or a funny moment that makes you giggle.

Even when the road feels long or slow, God is walking with you. He's in the laughter, the lessons, and even the quiet moments.

When your heart stays thankful, your journey shines with joy — every single step.

Creative Activity: *"Joy Steps"*
You'll need:
paper, crayons, and scissors.
1. Trace your footprints (or draw some big shoe prints!) on paper.
2. On each one, write or draw something that brings you joy — big or small.

JOY IN THE JOURNEY

3. Tape your Joy Steps along a wall or floor to remind you that joy follows you wherever you go!

Think and Shine:
What makes you smile even on an ordinary day?

How can you notice God's joy around you this week? What's one joyful thing you can do for someone else today?

Prayer:
Dear God,
Thank You for walking with me every day.
Help me see Your joy in every step — the happy ones, the slow ones, and the bumpy ones too.
Let my heart stay full of Your light and laughter.
Amen.

WEEK 35
LET JOY SPREAD

Bible Verse:
"A cheerful heart brings a smile to your face."
— Proverbs 15:13 (MSG)

Heart Talk:
Joy is a gift from God — and it gets bigger when you share it!

Have you ever seen how one person's laugh makes everyone else start laughing too?

That's what joy does — it spreads!

You can share joy by helping a friend, saying kind words, or giving a big smile to someone who looks sad. Even little things — like sharing your snack, or saying "thank you" — can warm someone's heart.

When we let joy flow from us, we become like sunshine on a cloudy day. God loves when His children spread joy, because it shows His love in action.

So this week, try to be someone's reason to smile. Your joy might be exactly what they need.

LET JOY SPREAD

Creative Activity: **"Joy Chain"**
You'll need:
colored paper, scissors, tape or glue, and markers.
1. Cut paper into strips.
2. On each strip, write one way you shared joy that day — like "helped my teacher," "played nicely," or "told Mom I love her."
3. Link the strips into a paper chain.

At the end of the week, look at your joy Chain — each link shows a moment you shined God's joy!

Think and Shine:

How does it feel when someone shares joy with you?

What are three ways you can spread joy this week?

Who do you think needs extra joy right now?

Prayer:
Dear God,
Thank You for giving me a heart full of joy.
Help me share it wherever I go — with my words, my smile, and my kindness.
Let my joy remind others that You love them too.
Amen.

WEEK 36

PEACE IN MY HEART

Bible Verse:
"Peace I leave with you; my peace I give you."

— John 14:27 (NIV)

Heart Talk:

Have you ever sat outside and listened to the birds sing in the morning?

Or watched the sky right before sunset when everything feels calm and quiet?

That calm feeling is a lot like God's peace.

It's what He gives us when we trust Him — even when things around us feel loud, busy, or confusing.

Sometimes we get upset, scared, or worried.

Maybe your friend didn't play with you today, or you couldn't find your favorite toy.

In those moments, take a deep breath and whisper, **"Jesus, please give me Your peace."**

God's peace is like a gentle blanket — soft, warm, and safe.

When you keep His peace in your heart, it helps you stay calm and kind, even when others are not.

PEACE IN MY HEART

Creative Activity: **"Peace Jar"**
You'll need:
A small jar or container, paper, and crayons.
1. Decorate your jar and write "My Peace Jar" on it.
2. Cut small slips of paper.
3. Each time you feel peaceful or calm, write down what helped — like "I prayed," "I listened to music," or "I forgave someone."
4. Add it to your jar!

By the end of the week, your jar will remind you that peace grows when you invite God into every moment.

Think and Shine:

What helps you feel peaceful?

How can you share peace with someone else this week?

When things get noisy or stressful, what can you say to Jesus?

Prayer:
Dear Jesus,
Thank You for giving me Your peace.
When my heart feels busy or worried, remind me to rest in You.
Help me spread peace to others — in my words, in my actions, and in my smile.
Amen.

PEACE IN MY HEART

A Bright Story with Miss Susan: "The Quiet Morning"

One morning, I woke up before everyone else in the house.

The sun was just starting to peek through the curtains, and everything was so still.

No phones buzzing, no TV, no talking — just the soft sound of birds singing outside my window.

I sat with my cup of tea and whispered a little prayer,

"Jesus, thank You for this peaceful morning."

As I sat there, I felt a warm calm fill my heart.

It wasn't just because the house was quiet — it was because I knew God was with me.

Later that day, things got busy and loud — breakfast spills, phone calls, and lots to do!

But every time I started to feel stressed, I remembered that quiet moment.

It reminded me that peace isn't about everything being perfect —it's about knowing God is right there, helping you stay calm inside.

WEEK 37
PEACE ON THE INSIDE

Bible Verse:
"You will keep in perfect peace those whose minds are steadfast, because they trust in you." — Isaiah 26:3 (NIV)

Heart Talk: Have you ever felt upset because something didn't happen the way you wanted?

Maybe a game didn't go your way, your friend didn't listen, or you lost something special.

It's easy to let those moments make our hearts noisy — full of worry, anger, or sadness.

But God teaches us how to find peace on the inside, even when the outside feels messy.

When we stop, take a deep breath, and remember that God is in control, our hearts begin to calm down — just like the waves of the sea becoming still after a storm. Peace doesn't always come from what's happening around us.

It comes from knowing God is with us, holding us close, and helping us stay strong.

So next time something doesn't go your way, whisper a little prayer:

PEACE ON THE INSIDE

"Jesus, help me stay peaceful inside."

You'll be amazed how His calm fills your heart.

Creative Activity: "Peace Cloud"
You'll need:
paper, cotton balls, glue, and markers.
1. Draw a big fluffy cloud and glue cotton balls to make it soft.
2. Inside the cloud, write words or draw pictures that help you feel peaceful — like "prayer," "music," "Bible," or "quiet time."
3. Hang it somewhere you'll see it every day to remind you that peace lives inside you when you trust God.

Think and Shine:
What helps your heart feel peaceful again when things go wrong? Can you think of a time you asked Jesus to help you calm down? How can you share that kind of peace with others this week?

Prayer:
Dear Jesus,

Thank You for being my peace when life feels stormy.

Please fill my heart with calm and trust every day.

When things don't go my way, help me stay gentle and strong inside.

Amen.

WEEK 38

PEACE THROUGH PRAYER

Bible Verse:
"Do not be anxious about anything, but in every situation, by prayer and petition, with thanksgiving, present your requests to God."
— Philippians 4:6 (NIV)

Heart Talk:
Sometimes our hearts feel full of worries — about school, friends, or things at home.

But God gives us a special way to bring peace back to our hearts: prayer.

Prayer is like talking to your best friend.

You can tell God anything — when you're happy, when you're sad, or when you're not sure what to do.

And the best part? He always listens.

When we pray, we're not just asking God to fix our problems — we're inviting Him to fill our hearts with peace.

You don't need fancy words or long prayers.

You can just say, "God, please help me feel calm inside," and He will.

PEACE THROUGH PRAYER

Every time you pray, you're letting God's light chase away the noise and worry — and in its place, He gives you peace that feels like a warm hug.

Creative Activity: **"Prayer Chain of Peace"**
You'll need:
Colored paper, scissors, tape or glue, and markers.
1. Cut long strips of paper.
2. On each strip, write or draw something you want to pray about — like "my family," "a friend," "my teacher," or "peace in my heart."
3. Link the strips together to make a paper chain.
4. Each day, pray for one link — and thank God for the peace He brings!

Think and Shine:
What do you like to talk to God about?
How does prayer help you feel calm or brave?
Who can you pray for this week?

Prayer:
Dear God,
Thank You for listening when I pray.

When I feel worried or afraid, help me talk to You and find peace inside my heart.

Fill me with Your calm and help me share it with others.

Amen.

WEEK 39
PEACE THAT STAY

Bible Verse:
"And the peace of God, which passes all understanding, will guard your hearts and your minds in Christ Jesus." — Philippians 4:7 (NIV)

Heart Talk:
Sometimes, life doesn't feel peaceful.

People we love get sick. Friends move away. Plans change, and things don't always go the way we hoped.

But even then, God's peace doesn't leave us.

It stays — deep inside — like a quiet light that never goes out.

When our hearts feel sad or afraid, we can close our eyes and whisper,

"Jesus, please guard my heart with Your peace."

And somehow — even if nothing around us has changed — we start to feel calmer, stronger, and safer.

That's because God's peace isn't just a feeling. It's a promise.

PEACE THAT STAY

It means that no matter what happens, we are never alone.

This week, let's practice keeping that peace — not only when life is happy, but also when it feels hard.

That's when God's peace shines brightest.

Creative Activity: **"Peace Lantern"**
You'll need:
paper, scissors, crayons, and tape.
1. Take a sheet of paper and write today's verse across the top.
2. Draw or write things that remind you of God's peace — like hearts, light, or praying hands.
3. Roll the paper into a tube and tape it to make a "lantern."
4. Put a battery candle or flashlight inside and watch it glow.

Every time you see the light, remember: God's peace still shines — even when life feels dark.

Think and Shine:

When was a time you felt sad or scared but found peace in God?

How does it feel to know that God's peace stays even in hard times?

PEACE THAT STAY

Who could you share this peaceful light with this week?

Prayer:
Dear Jesus,

Thank You for giving me peace that stays, even when things around me are hard.

Help me to trust You and remember You are always near.

Let Your peace guard my heart and shine through me.
Amen.

WEEK 40
SHARING GOD'S PEACE

Bible Verse:
"If it is possible, as far as it depends on you, live at peace with everyone."
— Romans 12:18 (NIV)

Heart Talk:
Peace isn't just something we feel — it's something we can give.

When God fills our hearts with peace, we can help others feel calm too.

We can speak gently, forgive quickly, and be patient when others are upset.

Sometimes, being peaceful means saying kind words instead of sharp ones.

Other times, it means choosing to walk away instead of arguing.

When we bring peace, we are being like Jesus —He calmed storms with His words and hearts with His love.

You can share peace by:
Giving someone a hug when they're sad.

Smiling at someone who feels left out.

SHARING GOD'S PEACE

Praying for people who are having a hard time.

Every time you share peace, you plant a seed of God's love —and soon, the world around you becomes a little brighter.

Creative Activity: "Peace Seeds"
You'll need:
paper, scissors, markers, and kindness!
1. Cut out small paper hearts or "seeds."
2. On each one, write peaceful words like "love," "kindness," "forgive," or "listen."
3. Give them to family, friends, or classmates this week.
4. Tell them, "Here's a peace seed — pass it on!"

You'll be surprised how far peace can spread when you start it.

Think and Shine:

How can I be a peacemaker in my home or school?

What does it look like to share peace instead of anger?

Who could use some peace from me this week?

SHARING GOD'S PEACE

Prayer:
Dear God,
Thank You for giving me Your peace. Please help me to share it with others — through my words, my actions, and my heart. Let me be a peacemaker, just like Jesus. Amen.

A Bright Story with Miss Susan: **"The Little Disagreement"**

One afternoon during playtime, two of my Sunday school kids, Emma and Noah, started arguing over who should use the blue crayon. Their voices got louder, and soon the other children began to look worried.

I took a deep breath, smiled, and said softly, "Let's all pause for a peace breath." Everyone stopped and copied me — we took one big breath in, and let it out slowly.

Then I asked, "What do you think Jesus would want us to do right now?"

Emma looked at the floor. Noah held the crayon out and said, "We can share."

Emma smiled and said, "You can go first."

In that small moment, peace filled the room again — like sunshine after a cloudy morning.

That day, I learned that peace doesn't always come with big words or lessons.

Sometimes it starts with a calm voice, a smile, or a shared crayon.

Lesson:
Peace grows when we stop, breathe, and choose kindness — even in small moments

WEEK 41
THE BEAUTY OF A QUIET HEART

Bible Verse:
"Be still, and know that I am God."

— Psalm 46:10 (NIV)

Heart Talk:

Have you ever sat quietly and listened — really listened — to the wind, the birds, or your own heartbeat?

Sometimes life feels noisy — school, friends, games, even good things can fill our days. But in the middle of it all, God whispers to our hearts. We can only hear Him when we slow down and listen.

A quiet heart isn't empty — it's peaceful, calm, and full of God's presence.

When we take time to be still, we remember that we're not alone. God is with us, guiding, comforting, and filling us with His peace.

You don't always have to do something to shine bright.

Sometimes the brightest light is the one that quietly glows — steady, peaceful, and sure.

THE BEAUTY OF A QUIET HEART

Creative Activity: "Stillness Jar"
Find a small clear jar or bottle.
Fill it with water, add a bit of glitter, and close the lid tightly.
Shake it up and watch the glitter swirl like all your busy thoughts.
Then let it settle — just like your heart when you spend time with God.

Prayer:
Dear Lord,
Teach me to be still and rest in You.
When my heart feels busy or loud, Help me find peace in Your quiet love.
Let my calm spirit shine Your light wherever I go.
Amen.

WEEK 42
THE POWER OF LISTENING TO GOD'S VOICE

Bible Verse:
"My sheep listen to my voice; I know them, and they follow me."
— John 10:27 (NIV)

Heart Talk:
Have you ever had someone call your name in a crowd — and you knew right away who it was, even before you saw them?

That's because love recognizes love.

God speaks to us every day — not always with loud words, but through gentle nudges in our hearts, through His Word, through peace, and sometimes through other people's kindness.

When we take time to listen, God helps us

know what's right, where to go, and how to love others better.

The more we listen to Him, the easier it becomes to recognize His voice among all the noise.

Listening to God isn't about being perfect — it's about being willing.

When we pause and say, "Lord, I'm listening," our hearts become tuned to His melody.

THE POWER OF LISTENING TO GOD'S VOICE

Creative Activity: *"God's Whisper Journal"*

Decorate a small notebook or a few pages of paper.

Each day this week, write or draw something that you think God might be teaching or reminding you.

It could be a verse, a word like "peace," or even something you felt in prayer.

At the end of the week, look back and see how God has been speaking to your heart.

Prayer:

Dear Jesus,

Help me to hear Your voice in the quiet moments and even in the busy ones.

Teach me to listen with my heart and to follow You with trust and joy.

Let Your words guide my steps every day.

Amen.

WEEK 43
WALKING IN GOD'S WAY

Bible Verse: "Trust in the Lord with all your heart and lean not on your own understanding; in all your ways submit to him, and he will make your paths straight." — Proverbs 3:5–6 (NIV)

Heart Talk: Sometimes God asks us to do things that don't make sense right away — like being kind to someone who wasn't kind to us, or choosing to tell the truth even when it's hard.

That's called obedience — doing what God says because we trust His heart.

When we obey, we're saying, "God, I believe You know what's best for me."

And each time we follow His way, even in small choices, our faith grows stronger and our hearts grow brighter.

God doesn't ask for perfection — just trust.

Even when the path feels uncertain, His love is steady and sure.

When we walk with Him, we never walk alone.

WALKING IN GOD'S WAY

Creative Activity: "Path of Trust"

Draw a winding path on paper that leads to a big heart labeled "God's Way."

Along the path, write or draw small acts of obedience you can do — like help a friend, say thank you, pray before bed, share your toy, forgive someone.

Each day this week, try one and color that step on your path!

Prayer:

Dear Lord,
Help me to listen and follow Your voice, even when I don't understand everything.
Teach me to walk in Your way with joy, and to trust that You always lead me right.
Amen.

WEEK 44
FAITH EVEN WHEN ITS HARD

Bible Verse:
"For we walk by faith, not by sight."
— 2 Corinthians 5:7 (KJV)

Heart Talk: Sometimes things don't go the way we hope — we pray and wait, but it seems like nothing is changing.

In those moments, it's easy to wonder, "Did God forget about me?

" But faith means trusting even when we can't see what God is doing.

It's like planting a seed — you don't see it growing underground, but you trust that something beautiful is happening.

God never forgets His promises.

Even in the quiet or hard times, He's working behind the scenes, shaping our hearts, teaching us patience, and preparing something good.

Faith isn't just believing when everything feels easy — it's holding on when it's not.

And every time we do, our light grows stronger and steadier.

FAITH EVEN WHEN ITS HARD

Creative Activity: *"Faith Flower Pot"*
Find a small cup or pot (or draw one on paper).
Write "Faith" on it.
Then, plant a small seed or draw one — something tiny that will grow.
Each day this week, water it or color it a little more as you thank God for what He's growing in your life — even what you can't see yet!

Prayer:
Dear God,
Thank You for being with me even when life feels hard.
Help me to trust You when I can't see what's ahead.
Grow my faith like a seed — strong, steady, and full of hope.
Amen.

WEEK 45

GOD'S PROMISE NEVER FAIL

Bible Verse:
"The Lord always keeps His promises; He is faithful in all He does."
— Psalm 145:13 (NLT)

Heart Talk: Have you ever made a promise — maybe to play with a friend or help Mom — and then forgot?

Sometimes people break promises, even when they don't mean to. But God never does.

Every promise in the Bible is true — and He keeps every single one.

When God says He will love us forever, forgive us, and guide us — He means it.

Sometimes His promises take time to show. Abraham waited many years for God's promise of a son. Noah waited while the rain poured. But in the end, God always did what He said.

When we remember His faithfulness, we can face anything — because His word never fails and His love never ends.

GOD'S PROMISE NEVER FAIL

Creative Activity: "God's Promise Rainbow"
Draw or paint a big rainbow across your page.
On each color stripe, write one of God's promises —
"God loves me"
"God forgives me"
"God hears my prayers"
"God will never leave me"
"God keeps His promises"

Hang it where you can see it as a reminder that His faithfulness covers your life like a rainbow after the rain.

Prayer:
Dear Lord,
Thank You that You always keep Your promises.
Even when I have to wait, help me to trust that You are working for my good.
Let my heart rest in Your faithfulness every day.
Amen.

WEEK 46
TRUSTING GOD IN EVERY MOMENT

Bible Verse:
"Commit your way to the Lord; trust in Him and He will act."
— Psalm 37:5 (NIV)

Heart Talk:
Sometimes life doesn't go the way we planned — a game gets canceled, a friend is upset, or a big change happens at home.

It's easy to feel worried, frustrated, or impatient. But God asks us to trust Him in every little thing — even the small, everyday moments.

Trusting God doesn't always mean everything will be perfect.

It means believing that He is working behind the scenes, caring for us, and guiding us — even when we can't see it.

When we choose trust over worry, our hearts feel lighter, calmer, and brighter.

Even small acts of faith — like praying before a test, helping a friend, or being patient — show God we believe Him.

TRUSTING GOD IN EVERY MOMENT

Creative Activity: "Little Trust Stones"
You'll need: small stones, markers, and a small bag or jar.
1. On each stone, write one thing you want to trust God with — like school, friends, family, or your feelings.
2. Keep the stones somewhere safe.
3. Each morning, pick one stone and say a short prayer: "God, I trust You with this today."

It's a simple way to remember that God is always faithful, even in the little things.

Prayer:
Dear God,
Help me to trust You in every part of my day,
even when things don't go the way I want.
Thank You for being with me and caring for me in every moment.
Amen.

WEEK 47

COURAGE TO STEP OUT IN FAITH

Bible Verse:
"Be strong and courageous. Do not be afraid; do not be discouraged, for the Lord your God will be with you wherever you go."— Joshua 1:9 (NIV)

Heart Talk: Sometimes God asks us to do things that feel scary —like trying something new, telling the truth, or helping someone in need.

Faith means stepping forward even when we're nervous or unsure.

It's like walking across a bridge you've never crossed — you can't see the end, but you trust God to guide every step.

When we choose courage, God's presence goes with us.

He doesn't promise it will always be easy, but He does promise He will never leave us.

Every act of courage, no matter how small, is a way of shining His light to the world.

COURAGE TO STEP OUT IN FAITH

Creative Activity: **"Courage Footprints"**
On paper, draw a path of footprints.

On each footprint, write one brave thing you can do this week — like say thank you, share a toy, help a friend, or pray for someone.

Color them bright and follow your own path of courage each day!

Prayer:
Dear Lord,
Thank You that You are always with me.
Help me to be brave and step out in faith, even when I feel scared.
Give me courage to do what is right and shine Your light wherever I go.
Amen.

WEEK 48
SHINING BRIGHT THROUGH CHALLENGES

Bible Verse:
"In this world you will have trouble. But take heart! I have overcome the world." — John 16:33 (NIV)

Heart Talk:

Sometimes we face tough days — when friends are unkind, things don't go our way, or we feel tired and frustrated.

It's easy to want to give up or hide our light. But God reminds us that even in hard times, His love is still shining in us.

When we choose to keep trusting God and showing kindness — even when it's hard — our light becomes even brighter.

Challenges help our faith grow strong, just like a tree's roots grow deeper in a storm.

God doesn't promise an easy life, but He does promise to walk with us through every storm.

When we hold on to His light, we discover joy, peace, and strength that no challenge can take away.

SHINING BRIGHT THROUGH CHALLENGES

Creative Activity: **"Storm and Sun Craft"**
On one side of a paper, draw a dark storm with clouds, rain, and lightning.

On the other side, draw the sun shining bright.

Write this in the middle: "

Even when storms come, God's light still shines in me."

Hang it where you can see it whenever you need a reminder to stay strong and bright!

Prayer:
Dear God,
When things feel hard or I don't understand, help me remember that You are still with me.

Give me strength to keep shining Your light, and courage to stay joyful in every challenge.

Amen.

WEEK 49
PEACE IN GOD PRESENCE

Bible Verse:
"You will keep in perfect peace those whose minds are steadfast, because they trust in You." — Isaiah 26:3 (NIV)

Heart Talk:

Peace is one of God's most beautiful gifts. It's not just about everything being quiet — it's about feeling calm and safe inside, even when the world around us feels busy or loud.

Sometimes, peace comes when we pause and remember that God is near.

When we pray, listen, or take a deep breath, we can feel His presence — soft, gentle, and steady.

God's peace doesn't mean there won't be storms.

It means that even in the storm, your heart can rest knowing He is in control.

When you spend time with God — in prayer, song, or silence — your heart becomes like still water reflecting His light.

PEACE IN GOD PRESENCE

Creative Activity: "Peace Jar"
You'll need: a clear jar, glitter, water, and glue.
1. Fill the jar halfway with water.
2. Add some glitter and a few drops of glue.
3. Close the lid tightly and shake it.

The glitter swirls like our busy thoughts — but when you set the jar down, the glitter slowly settles.

That's what happens when we take time with God — our hearts settle, and peace returns.

Prayer:
Dear God,
Thank You for being my peace.
When life feels loud or my heart feels restless,
Help me pause and remember You are near.
Let Your peace fill my thoughts and guide my day.
Amen.

PEACE IN GOD PRESENCE

A Bright Story with Miss Susan: "The Little Helper"

A few months ago, I was tidying up the kitchen after a long day. My mind was full of tasks — laundry, emails, and all the little things that seemed to never end.

Just then, my daughter walked in quietly. She didn't say a word, but she picked up a small pile of dishes from the counter and started helping. I paused and watched her, a little smile forming on my face.

Her simple act reminded me that kindness doesn't have to be big or planned. Even small, quiet gestures — like helping without being asked — can bring warmth and light into someone's day.

We washed, wiped, and put things away together, laughing at the water that splashed everywhere. I realized that God often shows His love in these everyday moments — through little helpers, unexpected smiles, and simple acts of care.

Even when life feels busy or overwhelming, His light shines in the small things, reminding us that love and peace are always present if we notice them.

WEEK 50

JOY IN THE QUIET MOMENTS

Bible Verse:
"You make known to me the path of life; in Your presence there is fullness of joy." — Psalm 16:11 (NIV)

Heart Talk:

Joy isn't something we have to chase — it's something God plants inside us.

It grows quietly, even on days when we don't feel very happy.

One evening, after a long day, I sat in my living room with the lights low. Everything was quiet except for the soft ticking of the clock. I felt tired — not just in my body, but in my heart too.

I whispered a small prayer: "Lord, help me find Your joy again."

A few minutes later, I heard laughter outside. It was my neighbors' children playing, chasing fireflies in the dusk. Their laughter was so pure, so full of life — it made me smile without even realizing it.

In that small, ordinary moment, I felt something shift inside me. It was peace. It was light. It was joy — not because everything was perfect, but because God's presence was near.

JOY IN THE QUIET MOMENTS

Sometimes joy doesn't shout. It whispers. It shows up softly, in quiet evenings, gentle prayers, and simple things that remind us:
God is here, and His love is enough.

Creative Activity: **"Joy Lights"**
Use paper and crayons to draw fireflies or stars.

On each one, write something that brings you quiet joy — a hug, music, sunshine, or time with God.

Hang them on your wall or window as reminders that even small lights can brighten our hearts.

Prayer:
Dear God,

Thank You for filling my heart with joy, even in quiet moments.

Help me notice Your light in the small things and keep Your peace shining inside me.

Amen.

WEEK 51
FAITH THAT ENDURES

Bible Verse:
"Those who trust in the Lord will find new strength. They will soar high on wings like eagles. They will run and not grow weary. They will walk and not faint." — Isaiah 40:31 (NLT)

Heart Talk: Faith isn't just believing when everything feels easy — it's holding on when life feels uncertain. There are moments when prayers seem unanswered, when days feel long, and when our hearts grow tired of waiting. But faith reminds us: God is still working, even when we can't see it.

I remember a time when I was praying for something so deeply that it ached. Days turned into weeks, and I began to lose hope. Then one morning, as I watched the sunrise, I felt a quiet peace whisper through my heart:

"Keep trusting. I'm still here."

That moment reminded me that faith doesn't mean we always feel strong — it means we keep walking forward, even when we don't understand. God renews our strength as we trust Him, and He gives us wings of hope when our hearts grow weary.

FAITH THAT ENDURES

Creative Activity: **"Wings of Faith"**
Draw or cut out paper wings.
On each wing, write a word or phrase that reminds you to trust God — "Patience," "Hope," "Strength," or "God's Promise."

Hang the wings on your wall or window to remind you that God helps you soar above worry and fear.

Prayer:
Dear God,

When I feel tired or unsure, help me remember that You are my strength.

Teach me to trust You completely and keep believing even when I don't see the answers yet.

Renew my heart and help my faith grow each day.

Amen.

WEEK 52

SHINE ON!

Bible Verse:
"Let your light shine before others, that they may see your good deeds and glorify your Father in heaven." — Matthew 5:16 (NIV)

Heart Talk:

You made it — 52 weeks of growing, learning, and shining with God's light!

Over the past year, we've talked about kindness, gratitude, patience, courage, and faith. We've learned that God's light isn't just something we see — it's something that lives inside us.

Every time you love someone, help a friend, forgive, or smile at someone who needs it — you shine God's light into the world. Even small acts can brighten dark places.

Sometimes shining means standing strong when it's hard. Other times, it means being gentle and kind when others are not. But every time you choose love, you reflect God's heart — and that's the brightest light of all.

Never forget: you are a light bearer. You carry God's love wherever you go. Keep shining, even on cloudy days. Someone else's heart might need your glow.

SHINE ON!

Creative Activity: **"My Light Collage"**
Collect old magazines, paper, or drawings.

Cut or draw pictures that remind you of the ways you can shine — helping, smiling, praying, learning, caring. Glue them onto one page and write in the middle:

"I will shine for God!"

Hang it where you can see it and remember: your light makes a difference!

Prayer:
Dear God,

Thank You for helping me grow this year.

Thank You for Your love, Your light, and the joy You've planted in my heart.

Help me keep shining for You — at home, at school, and wherever I go.

Let my life always show Your love.

Amen.

SHINE ON!

A Bright Story with Miss Susan: "The Candle at the End"

A few years ago, at a small church event, we each held a candle in a dark room. At first, only one was lit. Then that flame was passed from one candle to the next until the entire room glowed with soft, golden light.

I remember looking around and thinking — this is what God's love does. It starts small, but when we share it, it spreads, filling even the darkest spaces with warmth and beauty.

That night reminded me that we never shine alone. Each of us carries a spark of God's light — and when we live with kindness, forgiveness, and love, the world becomes a brighter place.

So wherever you go, dear one — keep shining. Your light matters. Your love makes a difference.

And God's light in you? It will never fade.

www.ingramcontent.com/pod-product-compliance
Lightning Source LLC
Chambersburg PA
CBHW080746060526
44119CB00072B/158